LOOM

LOOM

SARAH GRIDLEY

OMNIDAWN PUBLISHING
RICHMOND, CALIFORNIA
2013

Original cover artwork by Alex Friedman
www.alexfriedmantapestry.com

Book cover and interior design by Cassandra Smith

Cataloguing-in-Publication Data is available from the Library of Congress.

Published by Omnidawn Publishing, Richmond, California
www.omnidawn.com   (510) 237-5472   (800) 792-4957
10 9 8 7 6 5 4 3 2 1
ISBN: 978-1-890650-78-0

for Emilio

portami il girasole impazzito di luce

CONTENTS

SHADOWS OF THE WORLD APPEAR

And what is the body itself, save image and form of the ship? nacelle and hull, and votive vessel, even to its median opening; formed in the shape of a hull, and fashioned on its curves...

—Saint-John Perse

Still the Lady could come to her senses. Cool as a nude or a pressed flower.

One surrealist described it as
a *light task*:
to slice open pages

of a newly-
printed book.

Though I admire the greening brass of my dragon-handled
letter opener, it is nowadays better to be *paperless*.

There are those who said
only something useless can be beautiful.

I won't say we no more have occasion
to open correspondence

but No servant can serve two masters Luke said.
Thoreau said the perception of beauty

is a moral test—and—How vain it is
to sit down and write

when you have not stood up to live.
Consider the lavatory, Gautier said: can where we shit—

arguably the most useful room in a house—
be beautiful?

The warp is vertical, qualitative, a top-down scripture.
Goldenrod and rocket (though rocket

roots in distaff: a stick that holds
the flax for spinning).

Weft.

Weft is horizon—auxiliary, ornamental, washing the gloss
with further reflection—crane redoubling

the call of her mate—rouging silver and wildly cold
the winter ponds of crossing flights.

Show her bottom's blush in the scalding bath.
Show a stout cloud

of rose talc
where she dries to fragrant abstraction.

Show us up to our waist in grass and water,
rushes carding the clouds apart

on the glass-looking black of water.
She has woven us in descriptionless dark

lifting philter, charm, and poisonous light.
Nakedness is only

being itself: an uncarved block
turned on its side

a first
and last bad habit.

Mirror, plume by plume articulating the path

of funeral, its plumes and lights, processional, its profiles

in the long liquid surfacing of those—look—

them—motioning there—black plumes, anonymous,

not flying but gently bouncing, not human, but drawing

across the imaginal some flapping, some softly

figuring line, some extended sense of touch,

or tact, some feeling for what

has passed away,

is passing through a watching mirror.

There was a coin or a clue

or a ravel of flowers

the sun had caught to show us where.

There was a framing of flood

in all its factoring threads: its worths,

its wastes, its round-about ends.

Mirror whose willowed margins made room for light.

Mirror for the shadows of a river's blowing spears.

There is a history of the Lady we cannot see: not the right side of weaving
        where the mirror's looks

        are patterned out. Not the marketable output
        of industry, but the wrong side
        knots—the buried

snakes—
Here is a world
the Lady never said:

        silences her stars
        tottered and imploded in

        black threads   she pulled through words
        long rows in which   her heart was turned
        to gall, gold, grass   and spotted fur.

Long bolts of cloth. Huge hoistings of self to stillness.
And there were long days

of wonderful listening. And infinite backdrops
beneath her hands.

To look becoming is never impractical.
To wear something becoming is to have one's appearance flattered

by something one has put on.
So far is the hollow of being evolved—

the importunate burn of appealed-to horizon.
A cove, its seaweed air—

sunning strands and gasses in pockets, glisten of rock
and rocking weeds.

I do not wonder what became of her. I can only
speak for myself. *You have expected of me*

things as impossible
as I have expected of you.

It isn't difficult to remember
how it went.

A wordless world would be a relief
until it expects you to see a horse.

Try to sing and stand where the aspens quiver.
The breeze will always

be almost there. Go back those few steps:
it isn't difficult to remember:

the wind will always shine as if
it loved its armored riders.

The gold wire partitions of cloisonné
have shut up something colorful.

Are you deaf to onomatopoeia, Child?
To decorate is at root to accept

or receive. A cloister is a kind
of clause and a clause

is a kind of conclusion. In the art
of champlevé, metalsmiths field

a fly-ball radiance.
Pelter they say, Pelter, pelter.

Let us then be saints, said the radical empiricist,
whether or not we succeed visibly or temporally.

There in the roughest chapel
I remembered:

attrition is less than contrition
because motivated by fear of punishment.

There are times I will read anything
I believe: like that slate roof comforting

that naked bulk of peninsula.
To keep him safe from pirate pursuers,

the rock, the legend says, opened
and closed around

Saint Govan.
If Govan is a corruption

of Gawain, then the saint is more
or less fictitious. The legend says:

You cannot keep count of the steps
as you climb back up from the chapel.

The woods feel best
when barely raining, when talking scarcely resumes

in the greater space
of holding still.

Maybe the tree frog is still itself, an in
and of its own.

But a small-boned token?
But a cold-blooded omen

in the re-befriending
afternoon?

She is one to read all patterns of sand.
She is one to collect what stinks and shines.
Like the slang for living sea urchins

Whore's eggs.

Or *Fairy loaves*

slang for their fossil remains.

Urchin, hedgehog, hunchback, horror.
The *whore's egg*:

monstrous.

But how is it fed?
In reality

the mouth-apparatus of the urchin
is continuous from one end

to the other,
but to outward appearance

it is not so, but looks like a horn lantern
with the panes of horn left out.

So the whore's egg can dwell
so it might dig a living hole

in stone
there are 5 tooth-like plates.

To Aristotle, this structure resembled
a horn lantern without the panes.

We can guess the virtue
of the missing horn:

thin enough to let a flame shine through
—real enough

to leave the flame alight in wind

Wick-light flickers through the animal horn. The Hermit makes his way with a lantern. Is he your *guru*—your *staretz*, *tsadik*?

What is it you would have of him?

With the visual sense, and auditory sense, discrimination is said to happen objectively. With the tactile, mechanically. With the sense of taste and smell, chemically.

Sometimes a *whore's egg*—

phylum *Echinodermata*, whose creatures (urchin, brittle star, sea star)
share a five-fold symmetry, or *pentamerism*—

grows larger than its dugout, at which point it is said to be
IN FOR LIFE. Then it must depend

on food drifting to it.

What range of tones are possible
in the phrase *See for yourself?*

It is hard to explain.
Bloom is a noun and bloom is a verb.

In the spiritualist regard we are all part
of early photography. Around about the prow

s[he] wrote
The Lady of Shalott.

It takes me a full summer to get
the whole of the poem by heart.

Till her blood was frozen slowly
And her eyes were darkn'd wholly

thought over
and aloud in the woods.

Who is this and what is here.

Footprints, fingerprints, the odd depressions.

Here.
Sweep down.

Wet your finger
and speak to the weather—

lightstrips of wind pinned around corporeal clothes.

It is cold tasting light in the mouth.

It is how you resemble a vessel.
How you come up against every wave.

THIS HEART IS DEPENDENT ON THE OUTSIDE WORLD

When men are set free from the womb, the primal spirit dwells in the square inch (between the eyes), but the conscious spirit dwells below in the heart. This lower fleshly heart has the shape of a large peach: it is covered by the wings of the lungs, supported by the liver, and served by the bowels. This heart is dependent on the outside world.

—from *The Secret of the Golden Flower*

A Phenomenon

keeps for years in a button gone missing, or brings something of the sea to the surface of combs and boxes. When we reach into its thoracic cavity, the organs of a butchered cow, for as long as they hold together, we call the *pluck*. Do not call the world a box. A coast is first a rib and then a shore. Violets are a woodland breathing. *Nakara* in Arabic is to hollow out. Nacre yields us mother-of-pearl, liquor concreted as inner shell, little tomb of aragonite bricks that rough up light as iridescence.

Anatomy

Inside is a museum of natural history whose walls are now and again transparent. An otter whips tight circles in her tank, confusing the sense of humors. Water sloshes the sides like joy, in turmoils of minute bubbles. Press a hand against the glass. To say *live animals* is to call up figures of those who are not. The expression *wall to wall* can mean radical, as well as comprehensive. A taxidermist works in the basement with meticulous ambiguity. There is the barn owl returning to the fullness of barn. And trays of glass or acrylic eyes.

Casement

Here is her hand again. Not precarious, so much as reprised. Outside the colors are slipping to shadows. Inside there is still some work to be done. Her weaving covers the retreating reapers as far as their gleaming visibility. If she presses a hand, that cooled and exploded star, against the mirror, out comes the rippling banner and its flower. Looking threads darkness in coming light. She is spinning this world inside the other. The river that windows the changing hour. The fed owl departing the barley row. The high winds shagging the tops of trees.

Charcoal

for Heather

Line of impure carbon and available time. Seam of transmutable sadnesses. In the square the archway opens into, a line will bank on diverse wings, curved in a shared falling, to come aground, shy of here, in a drawing of mysterious accuracy. Drawing stars, and drawing firs, gentleness draws so well there is no mistaking its way. Line of impure carbon and unfoldable time. Seam of translatable sadnesses. Close friend of the shadow play of blue. Friend who goes as bells in snow. What finds the residue of bone and willow and leaves the careful working in our hands.

Clotho

She cannot see what her older sisters have in mind. Gaze à Marie. They are distancing the substance of gossamer. She cannot imagine the length of the virgin's winding sheet but can feel her spinning coming apart in the blue space of Assumption. She is turning away from that sky. Connecting birthday, and alphabet, and raiment—all three—she is walking the woods for an open-ended beginning. She is looking out in the way of a radius—that specified distance from a center in all directions—looking out with the aspect of making that distance known.

Edifice

In the river's comprehensive reflection stand the tall, thin men who taught me Latin. Rumpled and shining, they smile at one another and exchange congenial handshakes. When I am always older in their repetition, the days seem more and more analogous. A silver edgeless river—noon and its pounding sun. The long hand of the clock sticks, spasms, resumes. I am called on. Light coats the high tuition. I am sight-reading a description of Dido's Carthage. Light climbs the Latin. This could be stalling or stopping for time; this could be writing to the honeycombs in which space holds time compressed.

Every Hollow Holds a Hallow

Between the master craftsman and the apprentice, indenture was the cutting apart—in zigzag—of identical versions of the binding contract. Around the bonfire's acrid spiral, you wonder about the axis, the iris, around which the curve will be widening. There is a ship, or there are ships, reserved for rising apprentices. A ship is a vessel larger than a boat. In a ship, people and goods go across a sea for various reasons I can't go into here. In the illuminated times of apprenticeship, one's craft derived from apprehension, the getting hold of something physical or mental, through a motion both glacial and elusive. It was the shape of things to come. A master craftsman took a bite reminiscent of a mountain range. It was a binding contract, whether covered in sunlight or rain.

Fathom

Compass rose of outstretched points. Rose like a red uncommonly quiet. House that has moved each night around dwellers unawake but dreaming. Continental drifts of lemon thyme. Old book of the blue spruce drinking. Early notes of the dun-colored dove. Knocks at the rim of the external ear, dusk for the ones who do not dream through it.

Father

You say to verify is when, by any means, you bring to light. I point to silver granules left behind on a tenable surface of then. You see silver in the word emulsion. I see a milky light, almonds crushed in water. You cross yourself and list in threes. I say *grain* inside and think whatever happens. Was it anonymity or truth or hope when early photographers wrote in place of signatures, *Sol fecit*: The sun made it. One seed, all its allied grasses. Brain before mind—someone conducts its restlessness in the low light between the singular and collective singular. Tell me the truth. Or say it is hidden. I said to soothe once meant to verify. You ask what is the negative. Is it love or music pulling whiskey from light. The one or the many things left on our tongues.

Font

A rowboat on a patient rack makes up the end of a childhood path. Last year's cattails snow the Sagaponack. Near the suck of mud and rushes, a field of a tuberous crop has flowered. Flash of aluminum keel, spider webs wiped from its idle hollow. Warm rain and sand and darkening soil. Electric eel that shook the pond. Brackish rose-and-copper water. Weathers fall through a gathering basket. To glean was to tell potatoes from stones. Duckblind. Crossword. Watermill. A word wheels by, *grandmother*, on long, red, deepening waves.

Grimoire

One helped undo the rippled look of things beyond the pane. One called for writing on the pane. One seemed to aim at suffocation. One promised the end result of breathing freely. One made use of iridescent wings. One said to drink from the mirror, while another took bowls and bowls of blood. One called for moss on top of blood. One required no words at all. One turned a black stone green with just one word. One made all the horses bolt. One crushed a shade plant for the end of a sorrow. One derived a forest from pendant ghosts. One was a spell for no more spells. For cutting them down, and letting them go.

Hretha

Burning sweetgrass fills the room. What is the last month of winter? A bird is hunting from the sky. Not science or longing will have turned his feathers redder. It was always the winter season that made them so. It is always a winter season when red is reddest for the mind. The windows are black behind the curtains. There is no other pattern of weathers and stars. There is an old goddess of Ice. There is a cold name for our mouths to shape the icy moonlight in her tracks.

Hymn

Through dust and dusk and words that fast in the dark between them, let a moon appear to lift us through the paths of interrealming stars. At Wolf Moon, moon after Yule, let the outworn habit shine like empty snakeskin. Cardea, keeper of hinges, show us the power *to open what is shut; to shut what is open*. Give us the howls inside the falls of snow, the tracks to thaw, the loosening ice and list of days, the rough caws, the worms and crows that turn and cross the earth, earth that knows or finds uncertain slopes to April, to the whole of Pink Moon, Egg Moon, rounded, to the ground phlox again coming wild—and alewives heading once again upstream.

Mirror and Labor

It musters gold from midnight oil. With the tensile strength of its own attractive disinterest, opens and crosses from there to here. Hangs above the wide and underlying waterslides. And has it appeared, in the end, to be rounded? Appeared, so as to be gotten round—returned at all its edges by the outmost convergence of losing and giving ground? As if squarely in the face had ever been a meeting option. As if the river had ever worked to hold your aims or image still.

Mused a Little Space

Black columns of cream and barley. Columns of water or time marked valuable. Her pose turns reclusively multiple. She is depicted as holding her own. She is known to hold a box of butter. And so on and so on and so on. You will get her, only smaller. Holding her own box, only smaller. Markets, you were what the rivers and highways wound down to, the exportation of a curse, a gleam refining currency. Who is this and what is here. Let him muse a little space. Here is a boat importing a body. Let her go like an animal into appearance. Glassy countenance, it is you she brings to town, you she bumps up silently to wharf.

O

A prairie comes up from an underwater memory. A hearth comes true in the crudest ring of stones. *The dead*, a dead poet wrote, *look on and help*. Let a dropped first or final O be the flattening urge of Anglicization. Queen Anne's Lace will round the meadow. Where bluebirds rust and bend the grass, we can repeat the name, *Ohio, Ohio*. This other side of solstice, it is yours, and mine, and anyone's deep and extinguishing summer. Not inside us or outside us but the obbligato pressing on between.

Ill at ease interposes a preposition into *malaise* as if to point to an actual place in the mind of translation. Lu Chi in his Fu of 303 A.D. put the waiting this way: *We knock upon silence for an answering music.* Everything starts out kicking. Everything dies inside some kind of song. Different musics respond to knocked-on silences: boats in loose percussion with docks—wings that whistle without the form of melody. What if knocking itself could answer knocking. Even the gods had need of a physician. We called the peony after him.

Pupil

You might pay it no mind, I said. Round dark, bright moss. Your call, you said,
I'm done. Shut well. Nailed up. Turned down. Rose up, bound hair, clocked in.
Broke up, looked down: what then. No mate. One plate. *The Moon* clipped out of
there. Shall one nurse none. Saint all. Love none. Deep owl. Gray swan. Go on.
White birch. Dear fog. Come in.

She Who Invites

Our first mirrors were found in water. Later we turned our faces to stones we polished, then metals we rubbed for answers. In modern mirrors our faces attend an unseen wedding of reflective coating and cooperative substrate. To face the world can mean different things. Enraged by the powers of his sister, Susanowo polluted her irrigation ditches and threw a flayed colt inside her guild of women weavers. One weaver bled to death in response to the desecration: she had stabbed a wooden shuttle inside her womb. Then Amaterasu—The Shining One—She Who Invites—shut herself in a cave and blocked its opening with a rock. The world went utterly dark. Not until she could be coaxed out of the cave by dancing and laughter would Amaterasu show her face again. To keep her here, to make her entrancement lasting, the gods have left a mirror in the tree opposite the opening of this cave.

Singing in Her Song She Died

The trope of a *swan song*, particularly of a mute swan turned songful, keeps its webbing hidden to protect the moving effect of its glide. Though a mute swan is less vocal than other swans, it will hiss, grunt, snort, and whistle. In the rigging of phonetics a *glide* was a sound produced as the vocal organs moved toward or away from the articulation of a vowel or consonant, for example, the "y" sound detected in the seemingly single-syllable passage through the word, *mute*. In *mute*, the "y" sounded out in the approach to "u" disclosed another syllable in the word, like something salted away that could now be savored, the silence surrounding the word was holding back another fraction. *Gliding* spoke of unpowered flight, of noiseless, smooth, continuous motion.

Some of What Shines

is below valuation, though the story of earnings works to attract you. Much of what shines is the ambient world, a bustle of light outpacing you. If gloaming is the same as ghost, a wedded coast of earth and moon, much of what shines is already archival. A photograph of bison skulls, our pyramid pile we ground to bonemeal. Bright corn in steady rows, the eliding hurry of train-light. Loblolly pines line up in the no longer cultivated field, select needles loosening in the lower ranks of shade. The red cockaded woodpecker dines on the cones. Though namely baring the material, a mirror once stood with miracle. Red streak of black gloss capping the drumming bird-skull. We must learn that slipknot again and again. Earth, a period looped in moon, thoughtful in turn with what it encircles.

Switch

Whistle of brittle humans, peacocks, and horses; I will listen. To storage organs, ballads and anchors, to gripping beasts and lowered gangplanks. *Cut me a switch*, writes the poet and walking-stick carver, *to whip old ghosts through sunsets to the morning*. Though May draws flowers from switching branches and sunset anneals the burial grounds. Though fall mashes apples, leaves, and stars. If you are afraid to go, if you are afraid to come. There is always Nemesis, evener of chance, older sister of anything that counts. It is her oil stone honing every wave. It is her garnets looming underground.

Tetralogy

There is a lining where creation meets creation, where the two are of one choosing substance. In this quarter of the year, the meadows are never at rest. The cloth is shot with indeterminate themes. Feeling the clear whips of absence, feeling the black grips of gold. Everything is interior unless it is not. If it is simplicity she wants, what could be more simple. Shell and web: they are both secretions. A soul could at last be looked for where the scrupulous body falls to pieces. She spends a day at the mirror observing rain, its downward trails on glass, and a day among the larches thinking. When the mirror cracks from side to side, bad luck takes up the room's reflection.

Tower

Every level of the tower has a hearth. The stair spiral, of cut stone, feels like a stalk, the helix from which red fire threads out at every level of the dwelling. An axed birch curls to ash. There is no time she knows that isn't tactile. What is spoken, what is woven, will have turned into world. As a whelk is turned by water, the tower is turned by wind. Their background takes the greater part. She does not question the facts of seclusion. The fires are there without her knowing how, or ever asking who it is who lays them.

Web

A solitary life is normal for most spider species, and so a male spider looking to make more spiders must go to some lengths locating a sexually mature and receptive female. It is said that pheromones secreted by a female along her draglines can aid the male with this working out of her location. The word *pheromone*, with respect to any creature, carves the air with arrows, compounding conveyance with urgency—a chemically composed *come on come on* coating the dragline with direction. In such instances where he encounters a female-made web pheromone-coated in its entirety, prior to any mating attempt, the male must first destroy the web in order to keep the female's signal from reaching other males.

*

Today and tomorrow will be coming in turns. Clearings could come, or
saturations. As one puts by bad wishes. Or as one remains their old dark harbor.
March snow comes steadily across the morning, and calm feels, if not concrete,
then something largely material. All thoughts refer to thoughts, light or dense
as omitted matter. Each annotation never seems to end. When you come to a
fork in the road, said the trickster, take it. The view through the mirror is old
as a keyhole. Winter is that face drifting into grass in shades too light to follow.

HALF-SICK OF SHADOWS

Why do some people fatigue themselves in endeavours to unravel such phantasy pieces as "The Lady of Shalott"? As well unweave the ventum textilem.

—Edgar Allan Poe

A twig puncture—a laying in of eggs
by the female gall-wasp—will produce in time

a lump beneath the bark.
Gall is used

"to sadden" other dyes.
Mordant binds with dye and gall

to fix the red
of madder root.

A man coins a word for the worship of virgins.

In the alloyed air of touchable things,

a man is rubbing his temples.

She is paid alright
to sit for the painting.

If he can get her to float,
fully clothed, in bathwater, it will this way

solve the problem: how to give death (its real aspect)
to the living subject. He is working so hard

her teeth are chattering.
Her pallor

his palette
(its vividness) is masterful.

That I had an early grasp of this—
that shapeliness

in the written word
required a solemn respect for ratio

—did never mean I would
master it.

In the elementary wing
of female teachers

graphite was a loose delight.
My lower and upper cases

looped over halves
cut by light-blue dashes.

She is aware there is
a double there.

How close
the world comes

to being his.
How closely his work

is enclosing hers.
On either side the river lie

long fields. They clothe the wold
and meet the sky. Who was there is gone

except the reapers, a river and
its riding armor,

a knight, a horse, and the moving mirror.

Report: intelligence. Report: explosion.
Rumor, evaluation, transcription.

She is aware
there is that world out there.

Tension in fog
is a sound unique to the detailed mirror. He says she has

a lovely face. She feels the detail
in the fog. She sees an armor

shining off her throat. And equally
a nameless boat

rocking at
the end of chain.

To "foil" a trace
or scent, one runs an
other over
it—

Here the illuminant illumines the subject:
a small magnesium explosion
where a flashlamp
startles the veil

He was on his way somewhere
when common Solomon's seal
took effect in him: the spaced
appearance of flowers

spaced as the harpist's
tuning pegs

The flyleaf invites
a touch of formality. Come to the spare page:
the imaginary world seems promised here. A flyleaf says nothing.
A dust jacket says something: Let nothing speak to
or touch
what the story truly feels.

.

The Lady will come to her senses. There is leaf enough
in languish, in the rabbit's drooping ears,
in the backing of a gem
with metal foil.

A camera is a waiting room—and looks exchanged
between living and dreaming—and a hole

to spy their turning apart.
One used to clean cloth by trampling it.

The trampler was called
the fuller.

She says the mirror is a foil. She sees the flower
sewn inside the flag. The mirror is

this wind-flapped cloth, is also the murmur
it makes of armor.

You can pull out the row where the pattern was wronged.
You can go back

over it: the habit finally shed the sparkled acre sold
lichen like a living snowflake

chipped off stone. If those were his hands

—if that is the sun—

here goes a mirror
of what is expunged. Here is a reaper

reaping early. The prickled lightness of her brain, relieving spears
of trepanation—

red threads of a kestrel's hunting song   *killy killy killy*

Lichen,
dissolved in

the ammonia salts
of piss

yields a purple dye
known in a dye-world

as *orchil*.

She grew up with a form of technology
called a record player. Each voice came about

by circumference.
Where the needle set devotion

on a scratch, the Lady listened
to the skipping sound:

From the bank
and from the river

He flash'd into the crystal mirror   *Tirra*

                                                        lirra

by the river
Sang Sir Lancelot.

Who is this?
And what is here?

Not a branch or a star
but a flower

named for its deep-toothed leaves.
Not for the wide-bright florets—sepals soft enough

and light
to loft each shell containing seed—

up to twenty thousand ovaries
dispersed on breeze

In the slow darks
of elected solitude, in the motions

she would otherwise
forget to make.

Flute of the honest part of fire.
Iris of a pried-open fist.

The textile glows
with wordless stuff.

With angles the shadows
made of stone.

ACKNOWLEDGMENTS

Thank you to the editors at *Black Warrior Review* for publishing the sequence "Shadows of the World Appear" (as "Lucida"), and to the editors at *Columbia: a Journal of Literature and Art*, for publishing the sequence, "Half-Sick of Shadows" (as "Camera Obscura"). Thank you to Crazyhorse for publishing "Casement," "Charcoal," "Edifice," and "Mirror, Plume by Plume." Thank you to Eleven Eleven for publishing "Anatomy," "Father," "Hymn," and "Switch." Thanks to Cerise Press for publishing the following poems online: "Every Hollow Holds a Hallow," and "Mused a Little Space," and to *Web Conjunctions* for publishing the following poems online: "A Phenomenon," "Tower" (which originally appeared as "From Hands That Love You to Your Hands"), "Grimoire," "Hretha," and "Tetralogy." Select poems from this book appear in *The Arcadia Project: North American Postmodern Pastoral*, Ahsahta Press.

Thank you to Carl Phillips, Omnidawn, and Alex Friedman. Thanks to Community Partnership for Arts and Culture and Cuyahoga Arts & Culture for the Creative Workforce Fellowship that allowed me to begin this book. Thanks to my family, friends, and students. Special thanks to my uncle, Christopher Gridley, and to Martin Beisly, who put me in touch with Tennyson by way of a few nights' stay at Farringford House, Isle of Wight. I could not have written this book without walking the Downs that summer. Thanks to the late great Theodore Enslin, poet and walking-stick carver, for lines I borrowed from "Witch Hazel" in my poem, "Switch." Thank you, Melissa, for being such an exceptionally wise reader and correspondent. Thank you for reminding me of Heaney's "earthed lightning of swans" and of H.D.'s "boxes conditioned to hatch butterflies." Thank you, Bob, for your friendship and light. Thank you for pointing to le signe and le cygne. Everything is connected to everything. We are here to dream with our eyes open.

MORE ABOUT THE AUTHOR

Born in Cleveland, Ohio in 1968, Sarah Gridley holds a BA in English, magna cum laude, from Harvard University (1990); an MAT in English from Tufts University in conjunction with the Shady Hill School Teacher Training Course in Cambridge, MA (1992); and an MFA in poetry from the University of Montana (2000). After six years living in Maine, she returned to her native city of Cleveland in 2006 for a visiting lecturer position in the English department at Case Western Reserve University, where she is now an assistant professor. With the support of a $20,000 Creative Workforce Fellowship in 2009 from Cleveland-based CPAC: Community Partnership for Arts and Culture, she took a partially-compensated leave from her teaching duties in the fall of 2010 and began work on *Loom*. The poems in this collection are shaped by Gridley's longtime fascination with Tennyson and Julia Margaret Cameron, particularly the years they shared as neighbors and friends on the Isle of Wight, UK.

Loom
by Sarah Gridley

Cover text set in Trajan Pro.
Interior text set in Garamond 3 LT Std.

Original cover artwork by Alex Friedman
www.alexfriedmantapestry.com

Cover and interior design by Cassandra Smith

Omnidawn Publishing
Richmond, California
2013

Ken Keegan & Rusty Morrison, Co-Publishers & Senior Editors
Cassandra Smith, Poetry Editor & Book Designer
Gillian Hamel, Poetry Editor & OmniVerse Managing Editor
Sara Mumolo, Poetry Editor
Peter Burghardt, Poetry Editor & Book Designer
Turner Canty, Poetry Editor
Juliana Paslay, Fiction Editor & Bookstore Outreach Manager
Liza Flum, Poetry Editor & Social Media
Sharon Osmond, Poetry Editor & Bookstore Outreach
Gail Aronson, Fiction Editor
RJ Ingram, Social Media
Craig Santos Perez, Media Consultant